Successful
Business
Growth

in a week

ROSS MAYNARD

Hodder & Stoughton
A MEMBER OF THE HODDER HEADLINE GROUP

Acknowledgements

My thanks go to my wife, Margaret, for her brilliantly ruthless editing; and to my business friend Brian Coyle for his creative sparks. Thanks also to Eddie Kyle from whom I have borrowed the phrase 'The Plus One Factor'.

Order queries: please contact Bookpoint Ltd, 39 Milton Park, Abingdon, Oxon OX14 4TD. Telephone: (44) 01235 400414, Fax: (44) 01235 400454. Lines are open from 9.00 - 6.00, Monday to Saturday, with a 24 hour message answering service. Email address: orders@bookpoint.co.uk

British Library Cataloguing in Publication Data
A catalogue record for this title is available from The British Library

ISBN 0 340 72077 8

First published 1998
Impression number   10 9 8 7 6 5 4 3 2 1
Year   2002 2001 2000 1999 1998

Typeset by Multiplex Techniques Ltd, St Mary Cray, Kent.
Printed in Great Britain for Hodder & Stoughton Educational, a division of Hodder Headline Plc, 338 Euston Road, London NW1 3BH by Cox and Wyman, Reading, Berkshire.

the Institute of Management

F O U N D A T I O N

The Institute of Management (IM) exists to promote the development, exercise and recognition of professional management. The Institute embraces all levels of management from student to chief executive and supports its own Foundation which provides a unique portfolio of services for all managers, enabling them to develop skills and achieve management excellence.

For information on the various levels and benefits of membership, please contact:

Department HS
Institute of Management
Cottingham Road
Corby
Northants NN17 1TT
Tel: 01536 204222
Fax: 01536 201651

This series is commissioned by the Institute of Management Foundation.

C O N T E N T S

Successful Business Growth in a Week will help you grow your business. The book identifies the principles and features of business growth to help you create the environment for success. The book then takes you through 10 easy steps to achieve business growth in your company. Go for growth with *Successful Business Growth in a Week*.

Why grow?

Ninety-nine per cent of businesses in the UK (about 3.6 million firms) have fewer than 50 employees. 3.4 million of these companies have between 1 and 9 employees. Fifty-three per cent of all private-sector employees work in firms with fewer than 100 staff. Indeed, only 20,000 companies in the UK actually have more than 100 staff. (Source: *Small Firms in Britain Report 1996* – Department of Trade and Industry).

Britain is a small business economy, and the success and growth of our economy is dependent on the success and growth of our small and medium-sized businesses. Large firms expand and contract in cycles, but it is the small and medium-sized business sector which holds the future for this country in terms of wealth, jobs, new products and services, new ideas and business growth.

But you are not going to grow your business because it is good for the economy! Why do you want to grow? After all, small is beautiful, and staying small is easy: operations are easily organised; you have fewer staffing problems; there is no need to find larger premises; there is no need to raise extra capital for investment; there is less of a legislative burden; and there is much less of the sheer hassle and bureaucracy of managing a complex business. Given all these reasons, it is surprising that *any* business manager or owner ever chooses to grow their business! Some business owners are quite happy to run their businesses just to generate income for a comfortable lifestyle for their families. So why grow?

The reason for business growth is a very human one and can be summed up in one word: success. We all want to succeed; we all want to achieve; we all want to scale new heights and beat new challenges; we all want to leave our mark on the world. We all want to be good at something, and some people (entrepreneurs, we often call them) want to be good at business. Not just good: the best! This book is intended for those people – owners, managers and entrepreneurs – who want success; who want to grow their business; who want to be the best in their field.

If you want to grow your company, read on. First, let me put a few more challenges to business growth in your path: see the table 'Challenges to business growth'.

Challenges to business growth

Business growth requires	This means
1 Customer delight	Good understanding of your customers, their wants and expectations; excellent products and services (see point 5 below); brilliant customer care; effective handling of complaints, queries and problems.
2 Sales growth	Customer delight (see point 1 above); excellent products and services (see point 5 below); new; better products and services (see point 8 below); new markets and new customers; effective sales and marketing.
3 Positive people	Great staff, a good working environment and excellent training; a well-organised and structured company.
4 Leadership and vision	Clear goals and plans understood by all; and action, leading by example.

5	Excellent products and services	Good research, development and planning; efficient production and delivery; effective handling of problems; good relationships with suppliers.
6	Effective management	Good systems of control and management with effective managers and supervisors; excellent business information.
7	Sufficient resources for growth	Good cash-flow management; effective management of resources; clear plans to present to banks and investors.
8	Innovation	A constant stream of new ideas for products, markets and services; an effective means of reviewing and testing new ideas.

All of these challenges will consume time, effort and cash in unimagined quantities unless they are properly managed. The growth of your business must be properly planned and structured if it is to be a success. This book will help you do this.

If, despite the challenges, you still want to succeed, and you still want to grow your business, read on.

A passion for growth

You want to succeed in business; you want to be the best; you want to grow your business. But there are many barriers and challenges on the path to business growth, and your will to succeed must not be daunted by these. Your passion for success must overcome everything that is put in your way. Before we proceed, therefore, let us check your resolve and test your passion for success. Answer the questions shown in the table 'Your passion-for-success self-assessment', for yourself and for your management team. If possible, ask your management team to fill the self-assessment in too, and discuss the results together.

Your passion-for-success self-assessment	You		Your team	
	Yes	No	Yes	No
1 Do you have a vision of what you want to achieve for your business?				
2 Do you have the full commitment of your management team to the vision?				
3 Do you have clear goals for the future of the business?				
4 Are you prepared to work as hard as it takes to achieve your vision?				
5 Are you prepared to take the actions necessary to implement your plans?				
6 Do you have the patience and the stamina to implement your plans and strive to achieve your vision?				
7 Are you prepared to raise the funds that will be necessary to implement your plans?				

8 Have you considered the risks that might lie ahead?				
9 Are you comfortable marketing yourself and your ideas?				
10 Do you have the frame of mind to keep trying, regardless of the barriers and the upsets that occur on the path to business growth?				
11 Are you prepared to communicate fully with your staff and involve them in the process of business growth?				
12 Are you committed to being the best; to excellence in everything that you and your company do?				

Before you take action to grow your business, you should think carefully about your passion for success. Do you really want to grow? Or does it just sound like a nice idea; fine words, grandly spoken? Review the checklist again. Do you really *mean* the answers given?

Eight or more ticks in the 'Yes' boxes in both columns show you have at least the beginnings of the passion you need for success!

The PACE of business growth

Business growth requires you, and everyone around you
(particularly your management team), to accept,
wholeheartedly, the four guiding principles of business
growth (PACE):

1 passion
2 action
3 communication
4 excellence

You must have a *passion* for your business and its success.
You and your managers must agree where you want the
business to go; you must set ambitious goals; and you must
put plans into action to achieve those goals. Passion is about
a desire to win; a total belief in the goals; and the
commitment to take all necessary actions to achieve them.
Passion is vision, leadership, commitment to customer
delight and overwhelming energy, all rolled into one, and
totally focused on the business goals! Without passion, and
the energy it brings, your business will never change.

Action is needed to implement the vision and plans to
achieve the goals. Fine words and mission statements are
not enough. Words must be put into action with vigour and
consistency to gain the credibility, confidence and
commitment of the workforce. You and your managers'
actions must always be fully in line with the vision and the
goals if you are going to convince everyone in the business
of the sincerity of your passion; persuade them to have faith
in your vision, goals and plans; and motivate them to strive
together to achieve the goals. Politicking, resistance to

change, favouritism and in-fighting will all act to stifle the passion for growth, and must be eliminated.

Communication must be clear and open. Everyone in the business must believe in your passion for the business goals. Everyone must fully understand the vision, the goals and the actions that will be needed to get there. Communication must be open and full: secrets and surprises breed distrust. Involve staff in setting the plans, and be open about the problems and barriers that lie ahead. With everyone committed to the vision and involved in the planning and implementation process, problems, conflict and resistance will be minimised.

Excellence. Not everyone strives to be the biggest, but everyone strives to be the best. Developing passion, action and communication in your business will lead to a culture of excellence, of continuous improvement, of striving for success, of continually seeking better ways of doing things, and of determination always to deliver customer delight. Sustainable business growth can only be achieved through customer delight, and sustainable customer delight can only be achieved through a culture of *excellence*.

How much of the four principles of business growth do you have in place in your business, and what will you do to fill the gaps? (See the checklist.) Only when these four guiding principles are accepted can the process of growth begin.

A checklist for the four principles of business growth

Principle	What you need	What you have/ what you will do
Passion	Leadership. Vision. Common goals. Commitment to customer delight.	
Action	Implementation of vision and plans. Behaviour and actions consistent with vision, goals and plans.	
Communication	Clear and open communications. Full understanding of vision, goals and actions. Involvement of all staff. Honesty about barriers and problems.	
Excellence	Culture of continuous improvement. Determination to achieve customer delight. Striving for success.	

Business success factors

Business growth does not just happen. It is not the National Lottery for firms – 'This year it's you!' It has to be planned and managed. In particular, a number of basic features need to be established in your business if growth is to be successful and sustained. Evidence for this comes from the 1994 Confederation of British Industry (CBI)/Department of Trade and Industry study of the 100 most successful companies in the UK. This identified the following *Competitiveness Success Factors*:

Winning UK companies:
- are led by visionary, enthusiastic champions of change
- unlock the potential of their people by:
  - creating a culture in which employees are genuinely empowered and focused on the customer
  - investing in people through good communications, learning and training
  - flattening and inverting the organisational pyramid
- know their customers by:
  - constantly learning from others
  - welcoming the challenge of demanding customers to drive innovation and competitiveness
- constantly introduce new, differentiated products and services by:
  - deep knowledge of their competitors
  - encouraging innovation to successfully exploit new ideas
  - focusing on core businesses complemented by strategic alliances
- exceed their customers' expectations with new products and services

These 'success factors' boil down to the four features of business success:

1 customer delight
2 positive people
3 leadership and vision
4 innovation

To create the environment for business growth, you and your management team must wholeheartedly adopt the four guiding principles of business growth (PACE). This establishes the attitude and atmosphere necessary for successful growth. But you must also prepare your business for growth by establishing the features of business success: customer delight and positive people (Monday), leadership and vision (Tuesday) and innovation (Friday).

Summary: go for growth

There are no secrets to business growth, and no panaceas. Growth can be achieved through a practical and structured approach. Business growth *is* easy, but it requires you to wake up from complacency and shake off your familiar ways.

To grow your business, you must build a *passion* for your desired business goals and focus on them at all times. You must take consistent and determined *action* to achieve those goals. You must *communicate* your vision, goals and plans fully. And you must commit yourself, and those around you, wholeheartedly to *excellence*.

These are the guiding principles for growth. Only with your heart, mind and actions (and those of your colleagues) fully committed to these principles and to business growth will you begin to experience success.

Share the 'Your passion-for-success self-assessment' table on pages 11–12 with your team, and use it and the 'Checklist for the four principles of business growth' on page 15 as the beginning of your plans for growth.

When you have done this, go forward to Monday's chapter ready to start the process of business growth.

Customer delight and positive people

Introduction

Yesterday, we discovered that there are four features that need to be established in your business if growth is to be successful and sustained:

1 customer delight
2 positive people
3 leadership and vision
4 innovation

In today's chapter, we look at ways of developing customer delight and positive people in your business. We look at leadership and vision tomorrow and innovation on Friday.

Customer delight

Customer delight is the key to the success and growth of your business. Without customers, your business does not exist – no sales, no income, no staff, no business. *Everything* your business does, internally and externally, must be done with your customers (present and future) in mind.

This point seems blindingly obvious, yet enormous numbers of companies ignore or mistreat their customers. Customer care is frequently very poor in this country. I'm sure you can think of many more examples of times when you have been treated with arrogance, rudeness or contempt as a customer, than examples of your delight as a customer!

A 1995 survey by the Customer Service Lead Body
identified the 14 key features that customers (businesses
and individuals) seek from their suppliers. These were, in
order of importance:

1 reliability
2 fast response
3 understanding of needs
4 accurate records/information
5 confidence/warmth
6 active listening
7 ability to interpret information
8 honesty
9 knowledge of business processes and procedures
10 courtesy
11 product knowledge
12 value for money
13 assertiveness
14 maturity

Product knowledge and value for money (price) come surprisingly far down the list, and reliability, speed of response and understanding are the most important features in customer delight. Deliver these and you are well on the way to success – but not completely there: active listening, honesty, courtesy, knowledge and the other features listed are also very important.

Deliver customer delight and you deliver success and growth for your business. So what is customer delight, and what can you do to achieve it?

There are six elements to customer delight:

1 Understanding your customers' wants and expectations
Understanding your customers' wants and expectations is a two-stage process. First, it involves research into the markets in which you are operating (or want to operate) to fully understand the business environment. The market-research reports that are commercially available are excellent, and you may be able to loan them from your trade association, professional institute, reference library, university library, business development agency and so on.

The second stage is to speak to your customers. Ask them what they want from your products and services, and how you can improve. The very act of communicating with your customers is good in itself and will improve relations. Speaking to people you would like to be your customers is also good marketing. Ask them what they would like from your products and services, and what you have to do to make them your customers. It is not all about price. As we saw earlier in this chapter, reliability, fast response and understanding are often more important in customers' minds.

WHAT DO YOU WANT?

CUSTOMERS

Understand your customers' wants and expectations

Action	Your business
List the three steps you will take to understand your customers' wants and expectations	1) 2) 3)

2 Producing goods and services that satisfy your customers' wants and expectations

Understanding your customers' wants and expectations, and establishing good communications with them, is half the battle. It makes producing goods and services that satisfy your customers' wants and expectations much easier, allowing you to design in features that your customers want and to leave out features they are not bothered about, thus saving you money and making you more competitive.

Produce goods and services that satisfy your customers

Action	Your business
List the three steps you will take to produce goods and services that will satisfy your customers' wants and expectations	1) 2) 3)

3 Fostering good communications with your customers
Speaking to your customers should not begin and end with understanding their wants and expectations. It is an ongoing process. The cheapest and most effective way to improve sales is by selling more to your existing customers, and this requires good communications. Hold regular review meetings with your larger customers to ensure you continue to understand their wants and expectations. Survey (by telephone and post) your smaller customers so that you have good feedback on their views and have information that might be used to persuade them to buy more. Develop systems to ensure that you keep in regular contact with your customers.

Foster good communications with your customers

Action	Your business
List the three steps you will take to foster good communications with your customers	1) 2) 3)

4 *Customer care*

Customer delight is not just excellent products and services that do the job reliably and meet your customers' wants and expectations. It is also about the way your company operates. You must genuinely care for your customers. Good products are not much use if your staff are rude or indifferent; or your delivery performance is poor; or your invoicing is inaccurate; or dealing with your company is generally difficult. You must make every aspect of dealing with your company an easy and pleasant experience for your customers. Look at all aspects of your business from your customers' point of view. Simplify your procedures; train your staff to give excellent service at all times; improve your response to queries and problems; speed up your deliveries; give the best possible service. Customer care involves consistently making your customers delighted with the friendly, helpful, efficient face of your business.

Customer care

Action	Your business
List the three steps you will take to deliver customer care	1) 2) 3)

5 *Resolving complaints and problems swiftly and satisfactorily*

Part of customer delight is the effective handling of problems and complaints, and their swift resolution to the satisfaction of the customer. That doesn't always mean the customer getting their own way. It simply means an open and fair process with the outcomes explained at every stage, and any queries resolved. Most complaints and problems arise out of a lack of communication. Fostering good communications with your clients, and implementing good customer-care procedures, will help reduce this type of problem, but complaints will still arise from faulty products or bad service. These complaints should not be shunned. Customers who complain should not be faced with an implacable wall of silence – they will simply take their business elsewhere. Complaints should be seen as an opportunity to improve relations with your customers. If your company is at fault, apologise quickly and sincerely (the ability to apologise is a strength not a weakness) and rectify the problem swiftly. If you build your customers' confidence in your business, you will build a long-term (and profitable) relationship with them. This requires an effective complaints process.

Resolve complaints and problems swiftly and satisfactorily

Action	Your business
List the three steps you will take to resolve complaints and problems swiftly and satisfactorily	1) 2) 3)

6 The 'Plus One' Factor: standing out from the competition
To stand out from the competition and deliver customer delight consistently, you need to be different. You need to be better than the rest. What will you do to be better in this

way? This is the 'Plus One' Factor: the extra things you do
to delight your customers. The 'Plus One' Factor may be
achieved through well-trained friendly staff; or by following
up every sale to ensure the customer is satisfied; or by
personal attention to detail; or by rapid delivery/service; or
by free service visits to maintain good relations; or by some
form of customer loyalty scheme; or even by valeting your
customers' cars when they visit your premises. There are
many possibilities, and many types of excellence, but it is
important to make sure you have the 'Plus One' Factors that
your competitors don't by planning for them from the very
beginning.

The 'Plus One' Factor

Action	Your business
List the three steps you will take to develop your 'Plus One' Factors	1) 2) 3)

Positive people

How can you achieve customer delight without a motivated
and energised workforce? You can't! To deliver customer
delight, you need positive people – the second feature of
business success.

In a way, your staff are the internal customers of your
business: you produce a service (pay, conditions, working
environment and job activities) which leaves them either

satisfied or dissatisfied. Therefore, similar techniques to those used to create customer delight can be used to generate positive people.

There are six elements to positive people:

1 Understanding your staff's wants and expectations
Ask them what they want, and involve them in your plans for growing and improving the business. The people at the 'coal face' often have the best ideas for improvements. You'll find they want to help. Everyone wants to do a good job, and it's not in anyone's interests for the business to fail.

Understand your staff's wants and expectations

Action	Your business
List the three steps you will take to understand the wants and expectations of your staff	1) 2) 3)

2 Fostering good communications
Communication is the key. Once you start to communicate regularly and openly with all your staff, relations within your company will improve. Once confidence is built, people will open up and start to work together to achieve the business goals. Open communications lead to a better working environment, much greater awareness of the business and how it is performing, and to people dealing with problems as they arise rather than letting them fester.

Foster good communications

Action	Your business
List the three steps you will take to foster good communications with your staff	1) 2) 3)

3 Producing a service (pay, conditions, working environment and job activities) that satisfies the wants and expectations of your staff

Pay and conditions should be based on performance. Your staff deliver the customer delight that is the key to growing your business, and you should implement a profit-sharing scheme so that everyone can share the fruits of success.

The working environment is a more complex issue, but you can't expect your staff to deliver excellent products and services if the working environment is dirty, noisy and generally depressing. Clean up your act and make your workplace a pleasant, clean, safe, friendly and fun place to carry on business.

Similarly, you should ensure that people's roles and job activities are varied and interesting. Talking to your staff and understanding the other elements of positive people discussed here will help you do this.

Satisfy the wants and expectations of your staff

Action	Your business
List the three steps you will take to satisfy the wants and expectations of your staff through pay, conditions, working environment and job activities	1) 2) 3)

4 Caring for your staff

You expect your staff to care for your customers, so, in turn, you must care for your staff. This is partly linked to pay and conditions, but there are many other things you can do to show your staff you care (for relatively little cost): a company pension scheme, healthcare, child-care support, flexitime, nicely decorated premises, flowers or cards on staff birthdays, staff outings, team-building activities, and so on.

Care for your staff

Action	Your business
List the three steps you will take to care for your staff	1) 2) 3)

5 Resolving complaints and problems swiftly and fairly

There should be formal procedures for handling staff grievances so that an open and fair approach can be seen throughout your company. Just as you should make your disciplinary procedures clear and open so that managers' problems with staff can be resolved swiftly and fairly, so you should have an open and fair grievance procedure for staff complaints. In particular, managers should not be able to block grievances or act prejudicially against staff who make complaints (indeed, this could lead to an action for constructive dismissal through an industrial tribunal). Problems will always arise, and they should be dealt with honestly and justly, not angrily and summarily, if you are to retain positive people.

Resolve complaints and problems swiftly and fairly

Action	Your business
List the three steps you will take to resolve staff complaints and problems swiftly and fairly	1) 2) 3)

6 Training for positive people

A motivated and energised workforce requires investment in training to ensure your staff have the skills, knowledge and attitudes necessary to assist in the improvement and growth of your business. Common areas for such training include customer-care skills, problem-solving techniques, technical training, quality-improvement tools, people-management skills, team-building and so on.

Train for positive people

Action	Your business
List the three steps you will take to improve the skills, knowledge and attitude of your staff for business growth	1) 2) 3)

Summary

Customer delight and positive people are two of the four features that *must* be established in your business if it is going to grow. Customer delight is the key to the success and growth of your business, and positive people, an energised and motivated workforce, is essential to achieve customer delight. Both these features, as we saw, involve six different areas where you need to take action.

In tomorrow's chapter, we will explore the next feature of business success: leadership and vision. Innovation, staying ahead of the competition, is covered on Friday.

Leadership and vision

Leadership and vision is the third of the four features of business success. Without a vision of where you want your business to go, and of what you want to achieve, how are you going to strive for growth? And without leadership, how are you going to rally your staff and managers towards your vision for growth?

Leadership and vision embodies the four principles of business growth. Your *passion* for success and commitment to *excellence* provide your *vision* of business growth; and you turn your vision into reality by *leading* through *actions* and by *communicating* openly and fully.

There are five steps to developing the leadership and vision you need to achieve business growth:

1 create your vision: the growth plan;
2 lead by communication: proclaim the plan;
3 lead by action: implement the plan;
4 lead by openness: measure the results and communicate them;
5 revisit the vision: amend and revise the plan, and take corrective action as necessary.

The heart of leadership and vision, then, is the plan for growth, communicated to all, actioned and reviewed regularly.

Create your vision: the growth plan

Business growth must be planned, with every aspect covered, so that it can be achieved in a managed and co-ordinated manner. The *growth plan* is the manifestation of your leadership and vision, and provides the means by which you will lead your positive people towards success through customer delight.

The main elements of the growth plan are as follows:

1 the business background
2 the mission statement
3 the vision statement
4 business goals
5 the 'Plus One' Factors
6 strategic actions

1 Business background

The *business background* provides a short introduction to the company, its history and structure. It is the starting point for your growth plan, putting it into context.

Prepare your business background

Step	Your business
Describe, in a few paragraphs, the history and development of your company, including details of ownership, the structure of the organisation, size, location(s) and so on.	Your business background:

2 Mission statement

The *mission statement* is simply a short description of the products, services and markets that your company wishes to focus on. It provides a useful tool for identifying those products and markets which your business sees as crucial for its future success. Consequently, it can also help identify those areas which your company does not feel are profitable and wishes to withdraw from.

Prepare your mission statement

Step	Your business
1 What are the *products and services* crucial to the future success of your business?	Products and services:
2 What are the *markets and market sectors* crucial to the future success of your business?	Markets and market sectors:
3 What makes your company *special* in the eyes of your customers and sets it aside from your competitors?	Special features of your company:
4 Action: prepare a short mission statement for your company.	Mission statement:

3 Vision statement

Your *vision statement* sets the long-term (usually three-to-five-year) goals for your company. The vision statement should provide aspirational and stretching goals for everyone in the business to commit themselves to and strive towards. The goals should be clear and measurable so that performance towards them can be monitored.

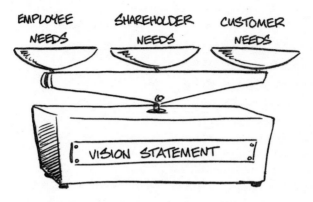

Your vision is key: it is what you are aiming for, and it provides the focus for all your passion, action, communication and excellence. In order to be successful in the long term, your business must balance the needs of three interest groups: the shareholders/owners, the customers and the employees. The vision statement should, therefore, seek to create shareholder/owner delight, customer delight and positive people!

Prepare your vision statement

Step	Your business
1 What outcomes do your company's *shareholders* or *owners* seek in the long term? More profit, more sales, higher productivity, improved morale? Less errors, less wastage, less lost orders, reduced absenteeism, reduced costs?	Long-term goals for *shareholder/owner delight*:

2	What outcomes do your company's *customers* seek in the long term? More on-time deliveries, faster service, better customer care, better quality? Less cost, fewer delays, fewer defects, fewer errors?	Long-term goals for *customer delight*:
3	What outcomes do your company's *employees* seek in the long term? More job security, higher wages, increased job satisfaction? Less hassle, fewer wasteful procedures, less bureaucracy, less 'us and them'?	Long-term goals for *positive people*:
4	Now combine the long-term goals of shareholders/owners, customers and employees into one vision statement.	Your vision:
5	Define the measures that you will use to monitor the progress of the company towards its vision; for example, size, market share, quality, customer satisfaction and profitability.	Measures of success:

Remember, the vision statement should provide a clear sense of direction for your company. It should engender team spirit and motivate employees to work towards this; and it should offer clear aspirational goals for shareholders/owners, customers and employees to aim for.

4 Business goals
The vision statement provides the direction for your company's business growth over the long term. The *business goals* are the targets that the company wishes to achieve in the current year as milestones to achieving the overall company vision.

It is important that these targets be *specific and measurable* in nature. Depending on the size and complexity of your business and the challenges facing it, your company should have between 4 and 10 business goals. To target more than 10 areas for growth can cause resourcing problems. It is better to focus on a small number of key areas at one time rather than to try to achieve everything at once!

Prepare your business goals

Step	Your business
1 Use your vision statement to create some short-term (one-year) targets for your organisation. Ensure that they cover the areas of shareholder/owner delight, customer delight and positive people.	Short-term targets:

2 Identify the main *forces* (external and internal) which are causing change in your organisation. These might include customer dissatisfaction, inefficient internal processes, changes in the marketplace, legislative or regulatory changes, new business opportunities, skills shortages, and so on.	Main forces causing change:
3 Select the most important of these forces and set *improvement targets* for them.	Improvement targets:
4 Combine the short-term targets derived from your vision statement with the improvement targets and rewrite them as between 4 and 10 business goals. Make sure that your business goals are specific and measurable, and set interim targets (e.g. monthly or quarterly) where possible.	Business goals and interim targets:

5 The 'Plus One' Factors

To stand out from the competition, and to deliver customer delight consistently, you need to be different. You need to be better than the rest. So how will you deliver customer delight? What will you do to be better? It is worth detailing in your growth plan the actions you will take to stand above the competition. These actions are the 'Plus One' Factors. For some companies this may be achieved through well-trained friendly staff. For others it may be a follow-up letter or telephone call after every sale to ensure the customer is satisfied. For others it may be personal attention to detail, or free service visits or a customer loyalty scheme. Make sure your business stands out from the competition by planning for the 'Plus One' Factors from the beginning.

Prepare your 'Plus One' Factors

Step	Your business
Write down the 'Plus One' Factors that will make your business stand out from the competition.	Your 'Plus One' Factors:

6 Strategic actions

The process of developing the mission and vision for your business, and of identifying your business goals and 'Plus One' Factors, will already have started you thinking about the *strategic actions* that you will have to take to achieve the business goals and, ultimately, your vision. Now we will identify these actions more formally. See the table 'Prepare your strategic actions'.

Prepare your strategic actions

Step	Your business
1 Review the *strengths, weaknesses, opportunities and threats* facing the business both internally and externally in the following areas: • products and services; • customers; • markets and competition; • sales and marketing; • management; • operations, processes and systems; • quality, and working environment; • finance, materials and resources; • people, skills and training.	Strengths, weaknesses, opportunities and threats:

2 Define the *critical events* that need to occur to achieve the business goals. These are the events/outcomes which *must* take place in order to achieve a particular objective.	Critical events:
3 Identify the *risks* that might hinder the occurrence of the critical events or the achievement of the business goals. Prepare *contingency plans* to deal with these risks.	Risks and contingency plans:
4 Define the strategic actions necessary to achieve the business goals, bearing in mind the strengths, weaknesses, opportunities and threats, the critical events and the risks identified.	Strategic actions:
5 Identify any additional strategic actions necessary to deliver the 'Plus One' Factors which will make your company stand above the competition.	Strategic actions to achieve the 'Plus One' Factors:

It is important to use *external data* as well as internal data for the review of the strengths, weaknesses, opportunities and threats of your business. Make comparisons with your competitors; review trends in markets and industries; compare technologies used with other companies; and so on. External trends and comparisons prevent the growth plan from becoming too inwardly focused and can provide fertile material for generating ideas for strategic actions.

Each strategic action (or group of actions) should have an identified 'champion' responsible for implementation, along with timescales for completion. Set targets to measure the success (or otherwise) of the action; for example, financial improvements, customer satisfaction levels and delivery or production targets.

List the strategic actions necessary for your company to achieve its business goals, using the grid shown.

Business goal:				
Strategic actions	Critical events	Targets	Timescale	Champion
Risks	Contingency plans	Targets	Timescale	Champion

Lead by communication: proclaim the growth plan

The growth plan is a living document guiding the development of the company towards clear targets. In order to be effective, it must be communicated to *all* employees so that they can commit their energies and efforts to achieving the agreed goals of the company.

To be communicated effectively, the growth plan must be concise and straightforward. It is worthwhile using several channels to communicate the growth plan to make sure the message is widely understood. These might include individual copies of the plan, company presentations, staff meetings, newsletters, posters and so on.

Step Eight on the path to business growth in Thursday's chapter provides more detail on proclaiming the growth plan.

Lead by action: implement the plan

Words are easy, but it is through action that the leader shines. True leadership and vision can only be shown by the vigorous communication and implementation of the growth plan. Managers must lead by example and act in accordance with the expressed vision and goals of the business if your staff are going to give the plan credibility and commit themselves to it.

Step Nine on the path to business growth in Thursday's chapter provides more detail on implementing the growth plan.

Lead by openness: measure the results and communicate them

Communication and action at the start of the path to business growth is not enough. People can get tied up in immediate issues and tasks and lose touch with the overall vision. For this reason, it is important to continue your communication efforts at regular intervals.

LEAD BY ...

COMMUNICATION

OPENNESS

ACTION))

Make sure you know yourself how you are progressing towards the business goals by measuring performance at least quarterly and, preferably, monthly. Keep your staff interested and energised to implement the strategic actions and achieve the business goals, by giving regular (at least quarterly) updates of results against the goals and the vision. Full, open and regular communications are one of the keys to positive people.

Step Nine on the path to business growth in Thursday's chapter provides more detail on measuring the results of the growth plan.

Revisit the vision: amend and revise the growth plan, and take corrective action as necessary

The world moves on, circumstances change, unexpected events occur. Your growth plan will not stay current for very long, so you must update it at regular intervals to ensure it remains relevant and credible. Quarterly management reviews and updates of the plan are the best way of making sure your plan continues to address relevant issues and takes you where you want to go. Communicate the results and revised plans to everyone to ensure all your staff remain focused on the business goals and vision of your company.

Step Ten on the path to business growth in Thursday's chapter provides more detail on reviewing and revising the growth plan.

Summary

Leadership and vision is the key to turning positive people into customer delight. To do this requires the focus provided by your growth glan. It is worth taking care with the preparation of your growth plan. A good growth plan, well presented and communicated, will help concentrate the energy and enthusiasm of all employees in the company behind the achievement of the business goals and the vision. After all, the business goals and vision provide benefits for staff and customers, as well as the owners of the business.

The path to business growth: the first four steps

So far, we have concerned ourselves with getting the prerequisites for business growth right. We have understood and adopted the four principles of business growth: passion, action, communication and excellence; and we have prepared the groundwork with three of the (four) features of a successful business: customer delight, positive people, and leadership and vision.

Now we come to the path to business growth: the steps you can take to grow your business.

There are 10 steps to business growth:

1 set up a growth team;
2 understand your customers and markets;
3 identify and measure key outcomes;
4 identify and map the business activities that deliver the key outcomes;
5 set the vision, business goals and 'Plus One' Factors for growth;
6 identify the main constraints to business growth and eliminate these;
7 develop the growth plan, and assess its impact on business operations;
8 involve and train your people;
9 implement the growth plan and measure performance;
10 review, revise and re-energise the growth plan.

We will cover the first four steps to business growth in today's chapter and the final six tomorrow.

Step One: set up a growth team

If business growth becomes the responsibility of just one person or department, it can easily become ghettoised and ignored by the rest of the company. It is important that your growth plan become accepted and understood by everyone in the company. This requires a growth team to communicate and action the plan throughout the business, and maintain momentum when other issues arise.

A good growth team will:

- comprise about 4–6 people drawn from throughout the business, including at least one employee representative if possible;
- commit the resources of its members to the implementation of the growth plan on a part-time basis,

thus giving them time both to action the growth plan and also to maintain their links and communication with colleagues in their own areas of work;

- include the most senior person in the company to give it the authority to implement the growth plan and overcome any internal obstacles that arise;
- be made up of people willing to take action to implement the growth plan;
- combine people of different backgrounds and strengths to give the growth team a broad mix of skills, abilities and knowledge;
- implement the growth plan fairly and openly in accordance with the principles of business growth and the features of business success;
- be subject to monthly accountability to the senior management team and quarterly updates to all employees to maintain full and regular communications.

The growth team should not:

- seek to intimidate others in the business or act in an elitist manner causing resentment and conflict;
- become a department in its own right with staff and overheads and every interest in promoting its own existence rather than the growth of the business;
- act in a secretive manner causing fear and uncertainty;
- seek to take the glory of business growth for itself. Positive people create business growth through customer delight. The growth team merely facilitates and co-ordinates the development, communication and implementation of the growth plan throughout the business.

Your growth team

Growth team member	Position	Key strengths in the growth team

Once the growth team is established, its members may require training to carry out their roles effectively. The training required may include:

- team-building
- effective management of meetings
- problem-solving skills
- quality-improvement (or Total Quality) tools
- people-management skills
- project planning and management
- communication skills

Step Two: understand your customers and markets

Customer delight is the key to the success and growth of your business, and everything you do must be done with your customers (present and potential) in mind. The aim of Step Two on the path to business growth is to understand your customers and markets. Bearing the six elements of customer delight (Monday) in mind, the growth team should carry out market research and speak to your customers regularly and extensively to ensure full understanding of their needs.

Understand your customers and markets

Understanding your customers and markets	Your customers and markets
Who are the existing customers of your products and services?	
What are their wants and expectations?	
What markets do your existing customers operate in?	

What other potential customers in these markets could you target?	
What would they expect from your products and services to buy them?	
What other potential markets for your products and services are there?	
Who are the key potential customers in these markets?	
What would they expect from your products and services to buy them?	
What new products or services might appeal to your existing and potential customers?	
What would they expect from these products or services to buy them?	

Step Three: identify and measure key outcomes

Understanding the present and potential customers for your products and services enables you to identify and measure the key outcomes that they want. This is important.

Customers do not buy your products just because they look nice or because they like your sales people. Customers also buy *outcomes* – they buy the combination of features and benefits that do what they want, when they want – and it is vital for you to know what your present and potential customers actually want from your business. In Step Three on the path to business growth, we identify the key outcomes that your actual and your potential customers want.

These key outcomes may include any combination of the following (this is not an exhaustive list, and there may also be other outcomes your customers want):

- fast response
- on-time delivery
- price (only one outcome, remember, among many)
- reliability
- brand image
- design

- technical functionality
- expertise of your staff
- friendly, helpful staff
- knowledge/understanding of customer's business needs
- convenience/location
- accurate and timely information, records and invoicing

Using the information collected during 'Step Two: understand your customers and markets', you should now be able to list the key outcomes that your current and potential customers are looking for in your products and services. Once you have done this, you should define the performance measures which relate to the key outcomes and judge your company's performance against these measures. For example, if you discover that on-time delivery is a key outcome, and that most of your customers want delivery within three working days of making an order, you have the performance measure for this outcome. If you measure your company's delivery performance and realise that you only manage to deliver within three days in 60 per cent of cases, you have a clear area for improvement. Similarly, if the technical expertise of your staff is considered a key outcome by customers but you only have a few field staff with detailed technical knowledge of all your products and services, you have a clear training need to improve your score against this performance measure.

You may wish to use more than one performance measure for a key outcome. Measures of customer satisfaction gained through surveying your customers or holding review meetings with them provide an excellent overall measure of the level of customer delight your business is achieving.

Your key outcomes

Actual/ potential customer	Key outcomes required	Performance measure	Performance target	Current performance

Step Four: identify and map the business activities that deliver the key outcomes

Now you know the key outcomes that your actual and potential customers want, and you have measures for those outcomes. The next step is to start improving your company's performance in delivering these key outcomes. This requires you to understand the internal business activities which deliver the key outcomes.

Each outcome is delivered by a combination of internal activities. For example, product reliability is a function of the product design activity, as well as of manufacturing, storage and handling activities. Your speed of response to customer requests is linked to administrative activities and procedures, the number of people involved, communication channels within the company and so on. For each key outcome, the growth team should list the internal activities of your company which combine to deliver that outcome. Then you should map those activities by seeking to understand the tasks involved in each activity, the time taken, the people involved, the interactions with other activities or people, and so on. Try to map the business activities for at least your top 10 key outcomes.

This is one of the most time-consuming steps in the path to business growth, but it is important to gain a thorough understanding of how the key outcomes are delivered and why there are difficulties in achieving the performance expectations of your customers. Bureaucracy or complex procedures, several people involved in carrying out activities and convoluted channels of communication are some of the main reasons for inefficiency in delivering the key outcomes.

An example of a business activity map

Key Outcome 1: fast response to customer enquiries
Target: response in 24 hours. Current performance: average response in 1½ to 2 days. Actual time to perform operations: 1¼ hrs to 2 hrs 20 mins.

	Business activity	People involved	Tasks	Time taken	Comments/ delays
1	Switchboard takes call.	3 operators	Record messages on pad.	10 minutes to take enquiry.	Messages collected twice daily – delay up to ½ day to pass on.
2	Salesperson prepares customer quote.	2 salespeople	Salesperson consults manuals and specifications to prepare quote sheet.	45 minutes per quote.	Messages left on desk if not in – delay up to ½ day to deal with enquiry.
3	Sales manager approves quote.	1 sales manager	Manager checks and signs quote and passes it back to salesperson.	10 minutes to check and sign quote.	Quote sheets left on manager's desk if not available – delay up to ½ day.

4a Quote approved and passed to salesperson.	2 salespeople	Salesperson faxes quote to customer.	10 minutes to fax quote.	Approved quote left on salesperson's desk if not available – delay up to ½ day.
4b Quote not approved and passed back to salesperson for correction.	2 salespeople	Salesperson revises quote and passes it to manager for approval (return to Step 3).	45 minutes to revise quote.	Quote for revision left on salesperson's desk if not available – delay up to ½ day.

Key Outcome 2: deliver product on time

Target: delivery within 3 days. Current performance: average delivery in 4–5 days. Actual time to perform operations: approximately 2 days 3½ hours.

	Business activity	People involved	Tasks	Time taken	Comments/ delays
1	Switchboard takes order.	3 operators	Record messages on pad.	10 minutes to take order.	Messages collected twice daily – delay up to ½ day to pass on.
2	Production planner schedules orders for manufacture.	1 production planner	Prepare production schedule for next day; and draft schedule for next week.	3 hours to prepare next day's schedule.	Schedule held until end of day before passing to operations manager – delay ½ day.
3	Materials requisition.	1 production manager	Production manager prepares materials requisition for store.	2 hours to prepare requisition.	Materials requisition passed directly to store. No delay.
4	Manufacture of product.	1 manufacturing manager; 10 staff	Manufacture of product through 6 stages.	1 day to manufacture.	Product passed to Finished Goods Store for checking. No delay.

5	Product checked.	2 quality controllers	Product check for faults.	15 minutes to check product.	Product released ready for delivery every half day – delay up to ½ day.
6	Delivery to client.	3 delivery drivers	Product delivered.	Delivery takes up to 4 hours.	Product only delivered when a suitable load is available for that route – up to 3 days' delay.

The book *Successful Process Management in a Week* by
Michael Tucker in this Institute of Management series
describes the task of mapping business activities in more
detail.

Summary

There are 10 steps to business growth, and today we have
covered the first four of these:

1 set up the growth team;
2 understand your customers and markets;
3 identify and measure key outcomes;
4 identify and map the business activities that deliver
  the key outcomes.

These first four steps on the path to business growth
involve a fair amount of research and preparation, but they
are essential to set the foundation for the final six steps and
achieve sustained business growth.

The path to business growth: the final six steps

Introduction

As we saw, there are 10 steps on the path to business growth:

1 set up a growth team;
2 understand your customers and markets;
3 identify and measure key outcomes;
4 identify and map the business activities that deliver the key outcomes;
5 set the vision, business goals and 'Plus One' Factors for growth;
6 identify the main constraints to business growth and eliminate these;
7 develop the growth plan, and assess its impact on business operations;
8 involve and train your people;
9 implement the growth plan and measure performance;
10 review, revise and re-energise the growth plan.

Today we cover the final six of these steps to enable you to complete and implement your plan for business growth.

Step Five: set the vision, business goals and 'Plus One' Factors for growth

You should now be beginning to see real progress on your journey towards business growth. You have set up a strong and balanced growth team, and this team has co-ordinated the effort to understand your customers and markets. The information arising out of this effort has been used to identify the key outcomes your actual and potential customers want, and you have measured your performance against these key outcomes. Next, you analysed and mapped the business activities which deliver the key outcomes in order to understand them fully and identify potential areas for improvement.

Now you are ready to start work on your business' growth plan. This work will be driven by the growth team but may require inputs from many others within your business.

The growth plan is discussed in detail in Tuesday's chapter on leadership and vision. At this stage of the path to business growth, you should prepare your vision for the future of the business, your business goals for the next year, and your 'Plus One' Factors to stand out from the competition.

The following points are worth bearing in mind:

Vision

- Your vision statement sets your long-term goals for business growth. It provides the focus for all your passion, action, communication and excellence.
- The vision statement should provide benefits for the shareholders/owners of the business, its customers and its employees so that everyone can commit themselves to working towards common aims.
- The vision statement should include clear measures of achievement so that you can monitor progress towards it.

Business goals

- The business goals provide the short-term (usually annual) goals for the company as milestones to the overall vision.
- Like the vision statement, the business goals should provide benefits for shareholders/owners, customers and employees to work towards.
- The business goals should provide clear and measurable targets for everyone to work towards, including interim targets.
- Your company should have between 4 and 10 business goals.

'Plus One' Factors

- Your 'Plus One' Factors are the features of your business which make it better than the competition (or will make it better in the future).
- There are many 'Plus One' Factors you might choose to develop, including friendly staff, rapid service or delivery, follow-up calls or visits, customer loyalty schemes, knowledgeable experts and so on.
- It is worth making sure your business stands out from the competition by planning for the 'Plus One' Factors from the beginning.

Step Six: identify the main constraints to business growth and eliminate these

In Step Five on the path to business growth, you began your growth plan by preparing your business' vision for the future, business goals for the next year, and 'Plus One' Factors to stand out from the competition. In Step Six we identify the main constraints and barriers which stand in the way of achieving the business goals and vision so that we can eliminate them, or at least mitigate them. This is best done by the growth team as a brainstorming exercise pulling in relevant employees and experts as necessary. It is important to note that staff working in an area where there are potential problems often have the best and most practical suggestions for improvement because they know the processes involved, and their weaknesses, so well.

Constraints to business growth may include lack of skills or staff, inadequate premises or equipment, insufficient spare funds, poor information, poor relations with suppliers, and so on. Use the table on page 65 to identify the main constraints to achieving your business goals (and hence your vision). As discussed in Tuesday's chapter, critical events are those events/outcomes which must take place in order to achieve a business goal.

At this stage, it is not necessary to decide *which* ideas you are going to implement to eliminate or mitigate the constraints (that is the next step!). Rather, it is important to consider as *many* ideas as possible for the removal of the barriers. Improve your chances of identifying the best ideas by consulting as widely as possible at all levels of your business.

Identify the constraints to business growth

Business goal	Constraints/ barriers to achieving the business goal	Ideas for action to eliminate/ mitigate the constraints	Critical events	Constraints/ barriers to achieving the critical events	Ideas for action to eliminate/ mitigate the constraints

Step Seven: develop the growth plan and assess its impact on operations

Steps Five and Six lead naturally into the completion of your growth plan in Step Seven. Use Tuesday's chapter on leadership and vision as a guide to help you develop and complete the growth plan for your business. Focus, in particular, on the strategic actions necessary to achieve your business goals and vision.

When the growth plan is complete, the growth team should present it to the management group for discussion and approval. Before communicating it to the whole company, the growth team and managers should consider the impacts it will have on the business. Things are bound to change – restructuring may be required, equipment may need to be replaced, staff may have to be retrained. All these changes need to be planned for and explored fully.

Consider the impacts of your growth plan in the following areas:

- *products and services*
  - What new products and services do you need to develop?
  - What existing products and services will you discontinue or change?
  - What will these changes mean in terms of staff, equipment, premises and so on?

- *positive people*
  - What will the impact of your growth plan be on your people?
  - Explain the changes necessary, and prepare for them by retraining, restructuring and so on.
  - Communicate fully and openly to maintain positive people.

- *resources and utilisation*
  - The stocks, working capital and fixed assets used in your business are all cash tied up.
  - How will your business manage its resources and their utilisation during its growth?

- *supplier partnerships*
  - What changes will you make to your relations with suppliers to speed up and improve the overall service that your customers receive?

- *management and organisation structure*
  - Is there a need to restructure your business to ensure the success of your growth plan?

- *management information*
  - Do you need to improve your management and business information to provide the rapid, accurate and regular data you need for effective decision-making?

- *cash flow*
  - What impact will your growth plan have on business cash flow?
  - Do you need to manage and forecast cash flow more effectively to grow successfully?

Step Eight: involve and train your people

Business growth involves change, and people are afraid of change. Failing to fully communicate your company's plans and actions for growth will lead to uncertainty, insecurity and even fear. These fears and uncertainties must be allayed, and this is the purpose of Step Eight on the path to business growth.

You have already involved many of your people. Your growth team comprises representatives from throughout the business, and it has consulted widely in working through the path to business growth and developing the growth plan. Now it is time to communicate the fruits of that work. Now you must motivate and energise your people to implement the growth plan and achieve the business goals.

You must show leadership and vision by proclaiming the growth plan with passion to all your staff. As discussed in Tuesday's chapter:

- communicate openly and fully to *all* staff;
- encourage feedback and discussion, and deal with all questions and challenges openly and honestly;
- be concise, focusing on the main elements of the growth plan to gain understanding of, and commitment to, these from staff;
- ensure that the vision business goals and strategic actions provide clear and specific targets that everyone can strive towards;
- use several channels of communication to get the message through, including meetings, briefings, presentations, memos, newsletters, e-mail and so on;
- communicate regularly so that everyone remains focused on business growth, and keep everyone updated on performance and progress.

Training is another excellent way of gaining the commitment of your staff to the growth plan because it gives them the skills they need to deal with the coming changes, and, indeed, benefit from those changes.

Training is part of the communication process, and you should consider training activities which will involve *all* your staff in the growth plan. Such training *might* include:

- understanding the company's mission, vision, business goals and 'Plus One' Factors
- the growth plan and how it will affect individuals, teams and departments
- skills for growth:
  - customer-care skills
  - interpersonal and communication skills
  - problem-solving techniques
  - quality-improvement tools
  - people-management skills
  - team-building
  - technical training
  - job-related training

Step Nine: implement the growth plan and measure performance

Action is one of the principles of business growth. Once you have communicated the growth plan to your staff and carried out the necessary training, you must follow this up with prompt and consistent action!

Implementation involves managers and staff working through the strategic actions in the growth plan monitored and co-ordinated by the growth team. The strategic actions describe what is required and who is responsible for the action, along with timescales for completion. They also provide targets to measure the success (or otherwise) of the actions; and they identify any risks that exist and highlight the contingency plans for dealing with them. Managers must lead by example and implement these strategic actions in the spirit of the expressed vision and goals of the business if your staff are going to commit themselves to its success.

Measuring performance regularly and giving feedback is also important to keeping your staff motivated and involved in achieving the business goals. This is where targets and performance measures are important since these allow performance to be gauged and reported. Performance measurement should take place at all levels so that the people implementing specific strategic actions can review their own progress and take corrective action as necessary.

All the performance data collected should be gathered together by the growth team to update management at least monthly. Formal updates of overall company performance against the growth plan, and, particularly, the business goals, should be given to *all* staff at least quarterly, and preferably monthly, through staff meetings, newsletters, team briefings, charts on noticeboards, e-mail and so on.

Step Ten: review, revise and re-energise the growth plan

Regular updates of performance against the growth plan are an important part of Step Nine on the path to business growth. Step Ten goes beyond this update mechanism, providing a complete and regular overhaul of the growth plan.

Circumstances change, and your growth plan will not stay current for long. You must, therefore, have a system in place to review and revise the growth plan to ensure that it remains relevant and up to date. The growth team provides the ideal means for this, and it should be responsible for the three levels of review:

1 the monthly or quarterly updates (described in Step Nine), provided to management and staff, of performance against the goals and targets set in the growth plan. Corrective actions can be taken as a result of these performance updates.
2 a six-monthly review and revision of the strategic actions in the light both of emerging trends and of the level of effectiveness of the implementation of the growth plan during the first six months.
3 a major annual reissue of the growth plan, fully updated and amended as a result of working through the 10 steps to business growth again.

The major annual revision of the growth plan allows you to maintain its relevance. However, it is also important to maintain the commitment and motivation of your workforce. To do this, the growth team should also regularly revisit the elements of positive people described in Monday's chapter.

Full and open communication is the key, and you should continue to communicate the growth plan, and progress towards it, as widely and regularly as possible so that everyone in the company remains focused on the business goals and vision of your business.

Summary

Now the 10 steps to business growth are complete. Your business should now be well on the way to growth!

As we have seen, business growth is a combination of passion, action, communication and excellence – the four principles of business growth. In Wednesday's and Thursday's chapters, we saw how to translate these four principles into the 10 steps that any company can take to achieve business growth.

This is a practical route to growth. However, there is one final element necessary to complete the picture. Constant innovation will be required to maintain your business growth and keep your company ahead of the competition. We cover innovation, the last feature of business success, in tomorrow's chapter.

Business innovation

Introduction

In Monday's chapter, we discovered that there are four
features of business success:

1 customer delight
2 positive people
3 leadership and vision
4 innovation

We looked at means of establishing customer delight,
positive people and leadership and vision in your business
in Monday's and Tuesday's chapters. Now we come to
innovation. Innovation is the essential ingredient to build
on your initial successes in implementing the 10 steps to
business growth.

Innovation is important because it is what you need to
continue your success. Only innovation – the constant flow
of new ideas for products and services, and new means of
producing and delivering them – will keep you ahead of the
competition in the long term because, only by being
different, faster, more caring, and more responsive to the
needs of your customers than your rivals, can you maintain
customer delight in the face of constant challenges.

Who dares wins! Or put another way: who innovates wins!
Customer delight requires excellent products and services
which exceed customer expectations. But customers and their
expectations are constantly changing, so your company must
continually develop new products and services to ensure that
you keep on delighting your customers into the future.

What is innovation?

Innovation is staying ahead of the competition. It is the continuous development of new ideas and new ways of working. Innovation is 'all activities for bringing a new product or process to the market. It tends to be a time consuming transformation process which is both management and resource intensive.' (*Managing Innovation*, 1991, Jane Henry and David Walker (eds).)

This definition draws out a number of important points:

- *Innovation* is concerned with the act of *introducing* new products or processes, whereas *invention* is concerned with the act of *discovery*.
- There are two main types of innovation: *market innovation* and *process innovation*.
- *Market innovation* is concerned with the development of new products, services, markets and customers. Market innovation is new ways of doing things in the marketplace to delight existing and potential customers into the future.

- *Process innovation* is concerned with improving internal processes, systems, procedures, organisational structures and so on. Process innovation is new ways of doing things within the business to improve the efficiency and effectiveness of your business.
- Innovation in business rarely involves amazing new discoveries or bold inventions. Most business innovation comes from fairly small improvements building on previous experience and knowledge. Innovations also often involve applying knowledge, expertise or technology used in one industry or market to another industry or market.
- Because innovation is risky, failure must be tolerated. Research shows that successful innovation is a function of the number of attempts – i.e. the more you try, the more you will succeed (but you will fail more too!).
- Being a successful innovator, therefore, requires quite a considerable investment in time and resources in making attempts at innovation, many of which will be unsuccessful. You cannot tell in advance which projects will be successful and which will not. Therefore, you must make sure your attempts at innovation are well managed so that they do not become a drain on the business, but you should also tolerate failure – try, try, try again until you succeed!
- Knowledge is the critical factor in innovation. Without a knowledgeable, expert team fully committed to developing new products, services, customers and markets, you will not succeed.
- Marketing is also vital. Coming up with a great new idea is not enough. Unless you market it effectively (either internally for process innovation, or externally for market

innovation), your innovation will wither on the vine. The Betamax video was, supposedly, more advanced than the VHS, but the VHS was marketed better and took the market. Apple was way ahead of Microsoft with its Macintosh operating system, but Windows was marketed better and Microsoft now owns Apple. The West (and Britain in particular) has a marvellous track record in research and invention, but it is the Japanese and others who take the ideas, develop them and sell them brilliantly to capture the market.

Five steps to innovation

Innovation is part of sustained business growth, so it is not surprising that the four principles of business growth apply equally to innovation:

1 a *passion* to be the best;
2 *action* to keep trying (and tolerating failure);
3 open and honest *communication* with everyone;
4 a culture of *excellence*, creativity and continuous improvement.

Innovation is a creative process, and it cannot be totally analysed or controlled – there is a large amount of luck involved. If you create a good team of positive people working in a conducive and creative atmosphere, you will be part way there, but that does not guarantee success. You can assist the process of innovation by taking steps to establish a supportive environment in your business. The steps for encouraging business innovation are very similar to the steps to business growth.

There are five steps to business innovation:

1 set up *continuous improvement teams* co-ordinated by the growth team;
2 select and understand the area for innovation;
3 identify key performance indicators, and set targets;
4 identify and implement improvements, and measure performance;
5 move onto a new area for innovation.

Step One: set up continuous improvement teams co-ordinated by the growth team

Your company's growth team (Step One on the path to business growth – see Wednesday's chapter) should provide the overall direction and vision for innovation in your business. However, since those that work in a particular area or department often have very good ideas for improvements to the systems and processes they operate, it is also a good idea to set up continuous improvement teams in each section or department. Membership of these will usually be voluntary, but members will benefit from training similar to that given to growth-team members (notably in effective meetings, problem-solving and quality-improvement skills); and some of their working time (a few hours a week) will be allocated to the work of their team. Initially, only the most enthusiastic proponents of change in your workforce will join the continuous improvement teams, but as they devise and implement improvements, more and more of your staff will be willing to take part in them.

The growth team will co-ordinate the activities of the continuous improvement teams, receiving copies of their meeting minutes or action points and requiring formal quarterly or six-monthly face-to-face reports on progress and actions taken. The continuous improvement teams should have delegated authority to make changes to the systems and processes they are scrutinising (provided these changes are reported to the growth team). However, the growth team should review and approve more significant changes, particularly those which will impact on other areas of the business, or on customers.

Innovation requires broadness of view, experience and background. The teams involved should be multi-functional and multi-disciplinary, comprising a balance between ideas people and technical experts. They should include strategic thinkers, managers, supervisors and process operators all working together in an open environment to devise and implement new and better solutions.

Step Two: select and understand the area for innovation
The growth team should focus its efforts on innovating in the key areas of the business such as increasing the speed of response to customers, improving services or making the company easier to deal with. These areas will often be identified during the development of the growth plan. In particular, working through Steps Two to Six of the path to business growth will highlight areas where innovative improvements are needed.

The continuous improvement teams will be concerned with more local issues. There may be continuous improvement teams working in areas of market innovation such as new product development, marketing or customer service, but many of the teams will be looking at process innovations such as improving internal procedures or production processes. In general, since the continuous improvement teams are made up of volunteer staff members, they should be allowed to identify their own priority areas for innovation. In the long term, this will give the teams more motivation and a greater sense of their contribution to the overall success of the business. It is quite usual for continuous improvement teams to start with some seemingly trivial problems (which are nonetheless important to the staff in that area) such as improving the decor and facilities of rest rooms or canteens. However, buoyed up by their early successes, they will soon move onto more weighty problems with a greater impact on business performance.

Once the 'problem' or area for innovation is selected, the continuous improvement teams should spend time researching and defining the issue so that they fully understand the area in which they are to develop new solutions.

Step Three: identify key performance indicators, and set targets
Just as in Steps Three and Four of the path to business growth, you cannot truly understand an area for innovation unless you can measure and map its parameters. Measuring performance and setting targets for innovation and improvement is vital and will involve defining the key outcomes required by the 'customer' (internal or external) and mapping the activities which deliver those outcomes so that opportunities for improvements can be identified.

The performance indicators and targets set will depend on the area for innovation and the outcomes required. Speed, cost, reliability, quality, efficiency and so on are always good measures.

The growth team will also be concerned with identifying performance indicators and targets for the effectiveness of innovation within the company as a whole. Useful performance measures for determining the success of your efforts at innovation include:

*   *sales from new products/services* – the total income derived from products and services launched within the last two years;
*   *sales from new markets* – total income derived from products launched into markets penetrated within the last two years;
*   *sales from new customers* – total income derived from customers gained within the last two years.

These indicators may also be expressed as a percentage of total sales. Alternatively, gross profit can be used instead of sales to give a picture of the profitability of the innovations.

Other useful indicators include:

*   *level of repeat business* – a measure of customer loyalty and satisfaction. This is measured as the percentage of total income derived from customers who have been dealing with your business for more than two years;

- the *number* of new customers acquired, new markets penetrated or new products/services launched in the last year;
- *time to market* – the total time taken to develop and launch new products;
- *customer satisfaction* – identified by customer surveys, growth in market share, repeat business, and so on.

Step Four: identify and implement improvements, and measure performance

Action, of course, is critical to innovation, and working through the first three steps to innovation will help the growth team and the continuous improvement teams identify the actions they are going to take. These actions should be agreed by the teams and, if necessary, approved by the growth team. The actions should then be implemented.

The effectiveness of the changes or innovations implemented must be regularly monitored by the teams against the targets set in Step Three to ensure that their actions are effective, and that corrective actions are taken as soon as possible.

The overall success of the company in being innovative should be measured by the growth team against the performance indicators selected in Step Three.

Actions speak louder than words, but it is important that they be backed up with performance monitoring to inform future decisions.

Step Five: move onto a new area for innovation

Once improvements and innovations have been successfully implemented and have achieved the targets set in Step Three, the continuous improvement team or growth team has finished its job in respect of that particular innovation. Some ongoing performance monitoring may be necessary, but the team is ready to move onto a new area for innovation. Essentially, this involves going back to the beginning and working through the steps to innovation again.

In order to keep everyone involved energised and motivated for continuous improvement, it is well worth holding six-monthly presentations of the successes of the innovation effort for all staff. Details would be given of the improvements made, new products or services launched, new customers, the successes achieved and so on. Prizes might also be awarded for categories such as the most successful market innovation, the most inventive improvement, the most effective internal innovation, and so on.

Innovation, like business growth, is a journey of continuous improvement rather than a destination, and the five steps on the path to innovation will continually be trod by the growth team and the continuous improvement teams as the business grows and develops.

Summary

Essentially, innovation fits the same model as business growth. It is about passion, action, communication and excellence; and it requires positive people, customer delight, and leadership and vision to be effective.

This is well illustrated by Peter Drucker in his 1985 article 'The discipline of innovation', reproduced from *Harvard Business Review* in *Managing Innovation*:

> *In innovation, as in any other endeavour, there is talent, there is ingenuity and there is knowledge. But when all is said and done, what innovation requires is hard focused and purposeful work. If diligence, persistence and commitment are lacking, talent, ingenuity and knowledge are of no avail.*

While they do not guarantee successful innovation, the five steps outlined above in this chapter can be taken to create an environment for innovation and improve the likelihood that effective innovation will occur in a managed and focused manner.

Teamwork, in an open participative culture, with positive people, a clear vision, and a deep understanding of all areas of your business, are the keys to successful innovation. Once you have those in place, try, try and try again. Who innovates (and keeps innovating) wins!

Summary

A passion for growth

Business growth is easy – you can grow *your* business! You have to have faith in your vision, and you have to have a real *passion* to grow your business. Not only this, you must also *act* on it. You must do what you say you are going to do, and you must *communicate* your vision, your plans and your actions to everyone in the business to gain their commitment, understanding and involvement too.

Finally, you must commit yourself and your business to *excellence* in everything that it does. You must continuously strive for improvement and success; you must be forever seeking better ways of doing things; and you must be determined, at all times, to deliver customer delight.

A framework for business growth

Passion, action, communication and excellence are the
essential principles you must embrace to achieve business
growth. Without them you will get nowhere. However,
wholehearted acceptance of these four principles is not
enough. You also need a framework to guide your efforts
towards business growth. This framework comprises two
aspects:

1 the factors that create business success
2 the 10 steps to business growth

Business success factors
There are four features that need to be established in your
business if growth is to be successful and sustained:

1 customer delight (Monday)
2 positive people (Monday)
3 leadership and vision (Tuesday)
4 innovation (Friday)

Each of these features can be broken down into elements to
help you establish them in your business – see the
'Business success factors' table.

Business success factors

Customer delight	Positive people
1 understanding your customers' wants and expectations 2 producing goods and services which satisfy those wants and expectations 3 fostering good communications with your customers 4 customer care: leaving your customers delighted with your service and your company 5 resolving complaints and problems swiftly and satisfactorily 6 the 'Plus One Factor': standing out from the competition	1 understanding your staff's wants and expectations 2 fostering good communications 3 producing a service (pay, conditions, working environment and job activities) that satisfies the wants and expectations of your staff 4 caring for your staff 5 resolving complaints and problems swiftly and fairly 6 training for positive people
Leadership and vision	**Innovation**
1 creating your vision: the growth plan 2 leading by communication: proclaiming the plan 3 leading by action: implementing the plan 4 leading by openness: measuring the results and communicating them 5 revisiting the vision: amending and revising the plan, and taking corrective action as necessary	1 setting up continuous improvement teams co-ordinated by the growth team 2 selecting and understanding the area for innovation 3 identifying key performance indicators and setting targets 4 identifying and implementing improvements, and measuring performance 5 moving onto a new area for innovation

Ten steps to business growth

The 10 steps to business growth provide the means of establishing the four features of success in your business and achieving business growth.

The 10 steps to business growth are:

1   set up the growth team;
2   understand your customers and markets;
3   identify and measure key outcomes;
4   identify and map the business activities that deliver the key outcomes;
5   set the vision, business goals and 'Plus One' Factors for growth;
6   identify the main constraints to business growth, and eliminate these;
7   develop the growth plan, and assess its impact on business operations;
8   involve and train your people;
9   implement the growth plan and measure performance;
10   review, revise and re-energise the growth plan.

The Successful Business Growth in a Week Checklist

You are now well on the way to business growth, but to ensure that you continue along the right path, use the 'Successful Business Growth in a Week Checklist' regularly (see the table) to monitor your progress and plan improvements.

Scoring (partial scores are also allowed):

'To do'	0 points
'In progress'	5 points
'In place'	10 points

The Successful Business Growth in a Week Checklist

	Item	To do	In progress	In place
1	**Customer delight**			
	Customer delight is regularly surveyed using a variety of tools and measures.			
	The company carries out regular marketing research into customer wants and expectations.			
	The company has close and proactive relationships with its customers.			
	The company produces goods and services which meet customer wants and expectations.			
	The company has good ongoing communications with customers.			
	Customer care policies and procedures are in place, and their effectiveness is regularly reviewed.			

CONT.

Item	To do	In progress	In place
Formal procedures are in place to manage and resolve customer complaints and problems swiftly and satisfactorily.			
The company delivers distinct 'Plus One' Factors to customers.			
The company has strategies to continuously review and improve customer delight.			
Section total (90)			
Item	**To do**	**In progress**	**In place**
2 Positive people			
The company understands the wants and expectations of its staff.			
The company communicates openly, honestly and regularly with its staff.			
The company provides pay, conditions, working environment and job activities that satisfy staff wants and expectations.			
Policies and procedures are in place to ensure staff are cared for.			
Formal and fair grievance and complaints procedures are in place to resolve staff problems and problems swiftly and satisfactorily.			
Training needs are regularly assessed and implemented.			
Management and supervisory skills are continually being upgraded.			
The company continuously reviews its position regarding positive people, and improvement actions are taken.			
Section total (80)			

CONT.

Item	To do	In progress	In place
3 Leadership and vision			
Senior managers/directors are personally and visibly involved in generating and communicating the growth plan for the company.			
Senior managers/directors demonstrate, by example and action, the vision and business goals of the company.			
Senior managers/directors have a strong commitment to customer delight.			
Senior managers/directors have a strong commitment to positive people as a means of achieving the business vision.			
Senior managers/directors communicate regularly and openly with *all* staff.			
The company has a clear vision and specific business goals.			
The vision and business goals reflect the needs of shareholders, customers and employees.			
Strategic action plans are in place to achieve the business goals and vision.			
The company has identified its 'Plus One' Factors that make it stand out from the competition.			
The constraints and barriers to business growth have been identified, and plans prepared to deal with them.			

CONT.

	To do	In progress	In place
There is a formal growth plan in place which is regularly reviewed and updated at formal quarterly or six-monthly meetings.			
The impact of the growth plan on business operations, staff and training needs, has been assessed.			
The vision, values and business goals of the company are communicated to all staff on a regular basis.			
Individual copies of the company vision and business goals have been distributed to all staff.			
Regular team meetings take place.			
Managers hold regular updates of company performance for all staff to communicate progress towards the vision and business goals.			
Section total (160)			
Item	**To do**	**In progress**	**In place**
4 Innovation			
The company has established a growth team, and implements the 10 steps to business growth.			
The growth team is concerned with developing innovation in the business.			
Continuous improvement teams have been established and are active in making improvements to business performance.			
The company has a culture of openness so that employees are involved in business improvement at all levels and business issues are regularly and openly discussed.			

CONT.

The company actively develops new products and new markets, and monitors their performance.			
The growth plan has clear targets and strategic action plans for business growth, increases in efficiency, new product development, new markets and so on. The strategic action plans are implemented.			
Business performance at all levels is benchmarked against competitors, market leaders and recognised 'excellent' companies. Improvement plans are devised and implemented.			
All employees are committed to the company, its vision and its success.			
The company is constantly striving for excellence – to be better than the competition.			
Section total (90)			
Overall total (420)			

A score of 300 or more indicates excellent progress towards business growth, while a score of 200 – 300 suggests that you could grow more rapidly with a more focused approach. If you score less than 200, you still have some way to go to achieve business growth, and I would suggest you work through this book again and follow the 10 steps to business growth in your business.

Support for growth

You are not alone! Most business owners, managers and employees want to be successful and grow their businesses. This book can help you focus your efforts and achieve growth, but there are other sources of help, advice and support which you may find useful. These include:

- Department of Trade and Industry
- Confederation of British Industry
- Federation of Small Businesses
- The economic development department of your local council
- Institute of Management/Institute of Directors
- Trade associations, professional institutes and other industry bodies
- Chambers of Commerce
- Training and Enterprise Councils (TECs), Business Links, or, in Scotland, Local Enterprise Companies (LECs)
- Business Shops
- The Prince's Youth Business Trust
- The business and reference sections of libraries
- Business-studies departments of universities
- Advisory Conciliation and Arbitration Service (ACAS) for advice on employment issues
- The business banking departments of local banks
- Education Business Partnerships
- Local Enterprise Trusts or other local business initiatives
- Business clubs/networks

It is worth spending some time researching the organisations that are of most relevance to your business and getting in touch with them to see what support they can provide.

Summary

Business growth is easy! Every business can grow. You *can* grow your business if you only try. This book can help you, and there are many other sources of support available, but you must provide the passion and energy to make it happen. Now go and do it. Build customer delight, positive people, leadership and vision, and innovation into your business and follow the path to business growth.

With passion, action, communication and excellence guiding your every step, grow your business!

I wish you luck.